101

LOG CABIN BLOCKS™

101 Log Cabin Blocks
Index

101 Log Cabin Blocks is published by DRG, 306 East Parr Road, Berne, IN 46711. Printed in USA. Copyright © 2010 DRG. All rights reserved. This publication may not be reproduced in part or in whole without written permission from the publisher.

RETAIL STORES: If you would like to carry this pattern book or any other DRG publications, visit DRGwholesale.com

Every effort has been made to ensure that the instructions in this publication are complete and accurate. We cannot, however, take responsibility for human error, typographical mistakes or variations in individual work. Please visit ClotildeCustomerCare.com to check for pattern updates.

Printed in U.S.A.
Library of Congress Number: 2010917056
ISBN: 978-1-59217-335-8

2 3 4 5 6 7 8 9

Introduction

Everyone who loves Log Cabin blocks will love owning this book! Not only does it include the traditional Log Cabin block (in four sizes), it takes the Log Cabin out of the past and into a new creative realm of innovative block design.

We have twisted the logs and changed the usual rectangular strip shape—making this the most exciting collection of Log Cabin blocks ever! We've included new blocks where the logs become flowers, houses, hearts and even animals. We have definitely stretched the definition of a Log Cabin block being strips (or logs) added around a center square.

Using our foundation method for piecing, you don't have to worry about exact cutting of any weird shapes or tedious matching of points. Pieces are added to a foundation using a stitch-and-flip-open technique where all you have to do is stitch on the line. We have also included instructions for planning and finishing quilts using Log Cabin blocks so that you will be able to successfully complete your own unique quilt.

101 Log Cabin Blocks

A Little History

When one thinks about the history of the Log Cabin quilt, one usually thinks about the pioneers of the nineteenth century who lived in log cabin houses. The Log Cabin block was a symbol of their home. The strips were sewn around a center just as logs were built around a central hearth. The centers of the Log Cabin blocks were often red which symbolized the chimney as a source of warmth. Yellow was also commonly used in the center squares to represent the lantern as a welcoming gesture. The blocks were most often done with dark fabrics on two adjacent sides and light fabrics on the other two sides. They arranged the blocks in wonderful settings—some of which had their own names—Barn Raising, Straight Furrows, and Sunshine and Shadows. See illustrations on page 6 and 7.

The women made these utilitarian quilts from whatever material they had available—worn clothing, flour sacks, worn bedding and leftover scraps from their sewing. By making Log Cabin quilts, they made the best use of the fabric they had since they were able to use some fairly small pieces for the "logs."

About Our Blocks

The Log Cabin blocks in this collection range from the very traditional to the very modern. Five of the more traditional Log Cabin blocks come in four sizes, 4", 5", 6" and 7". There are also blocks that measure 6" x 8" and 7" x 8", but most of them are 7" square.

Foundation Piecing

The easiest and most accurate way to piece Log Cabin blocks is the foundation method. It eliminates the need to cut out each piece exactly.

Your first consideration is what type of foundation to use for piecing your blocks. There are several options. A light-colored, lightweight cotton fabric or muslin are popular choices. A lightweight fabric needs to be light enough to see through to trace onto and will give extra stability to your blocks. Of course, it will add another layer of fabric which you will have to quilt through. This extra thickness is a consideration only if you plan to do hand quilting. Another choice for foundations is paper. Use any paper that you can see through (notebook paper, copy paper, newsprint, or computer paper) for easy tracing, then tear it away after sewing is completed.

Mirror Images

Log Cabin blocks, in general, are not symmetrical, therefore a mirror image of the block pattern will be produced when pieced, **Fig 1**. On each pattern page (pages 12 to 116), there is a small diagram showing how the block will look once it has been pieced.

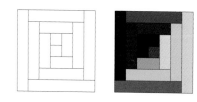

Fig 1

Note whether it is a mirror image of the block pattern and take that into consideration when choosing fabric and planning your quilt layout.

Preparing the Foundation

Tracing the Block

Trace the block pattern carefully onto your chosen foundation material. Use a ruler and a fine-point permanent marker to make straight lines and be sure to include all numbers. Draw a line ¼" from the outside edges of the block, **Fig 2**; cut along this outside drawn line. Repeat for the needed number of blocks for your quilt.

Fig 2

*Hint: If you want your finished block to have the same direction as the block pattern (for ex`ample, if you want the finished Log Cabin block #2 to spin in a counterclockwise direction rather than in a clockwise direction), you must first trace onto tracing paper, then flop pattern and trace onto foundation material, **Fig 3**.*

Fig 3
Flop and trace onto foundation

Transferring the Block

The block pattern can also be transferred onto foundation material using a transfer pen or pencil. Trace the block pattern onto paper using a transfer pen or pencil. Then, following manufacturer's directions, iron transfer onto foundation material. Write numbers on foundation using a fine-point permanent marking pen. The block, when pieced, will look like the pattern as it appears in the book, but will be a mirror image to the completed block shown in the color photographs.

Hint: If you want your Log Cabin block to look like the completed block shown in color and you are using a transfer pen or pencil (for example, you want the Log Cabin block #2 to spin clockwise), transfer as described above. But, if you would like your Log Cabin block #2 to spin counterclockwise, you must trace first with a permanent pen onto tracing paper, flop the traced design and trace again with the transfer pen or pencil.

Fabric

We recommend using 100% cotton fabric for piecing the Log Cabin blocks. By using cotton rather than cotton/polyester blends, the pieces will respond better to finger pressing.

Pre-washing fabric is not necessary, but it is necessary to test your fabric to make certain that the fabric is colorfast and preshrunk (don't trust those manufacturer's labels). Start by cutting a 2"-wide strip (cut crosswise) of each of the fabrics that you have selected for your quilt. To determine whether the fabric is colorfast, put each strip separately into a clean bowl of extremely hot water, or hold the fabric strip under hot running water. If your fabric bleeds a great deal, all is not necessarily lost. It might only be necessary to wash all of that fabric until all of the excess dye has washed out. Fabrics which continue to bleed after they have been washed several times should be eliminated.

To test for shrinkage, take each saturated strip and iron it dry with a hot iron. When the strip is completely dry, measure and compare it to your original 2" measurements. If all of your fabric strips shrink about the same amount, then you really have

no problem. When you wash your finished quilt, you may achieve the puckered look of an antique quilt. If you do not want this look, you will have to wash and dry all of the fabric before beginning so that shrinkage is no longer a problem. If only one of your fabrics is shrinking more than the others, it will have to be washed and dried, or discarded.

Cutting the Fabric

The beauty of foundation piecing is that you do not have to cut every exact piece for every block. You can use strips, rectangles, squares or any odd-shaped scrap for piecing. You do have to be careful to use a piece of fabric that is at least ¼" larger on all sides than the space it is to cover. Triangle shapes can be a little tricky to piece. Use generous-sized fabric pieces and be careful when positioning the pieces onto the foundation. You do waste some fabric this way, but the time it saves in cutting will be worth it in the end.

Hint: Cut strips the width needed for the spaces on the block. Stack strips in numerical order to make piecing easier and quicker.

Foundation Piecing

1. Prepare foundations as described in Preparing the Foundation, page 4.

2. Turn foundation with unmarked side facing you and position piece 1 over the space marked 1 on the foundation. Hold foundation up to a light source to make sure that fabric overlaps at least ¼" on all sides of space 1, **Fig 4**; pin or glue in place with a glue stick. *Note: Use only a small dab of glue to hold fabric in place.*

Fig 4

3. Place fabric piece 2 right sides together with piece 1. *Note: Double check to see if fabric piece chosen will cover space 2 completely by folding over along line between space 1 and 2, **Fig 5**.*

Fig 5

4. Turn foundation with marked side facing you and fold foundation forward along line between spaces 1 and 2; trim both pieces about ¼" above fold line, **Fig 6**.

Fig 6

5. With marked side of foundation still facing you and using a very small stitch (to allow for easier paper removal), sew along line between spaces 1 and 2, **Fig 7**; begin and end two to three stitches beyond line.

Fig 7

6. Turn foundation over. Open piece 2 and finger press seam, **Fig 8**. Use a pin or a dab of glue stick to hold piece in place.

Fig 8

5

7. Turn foundation with marked side facing you; fold foundation forward along line between spaces 2 and 3 and trim piece 2 about ¼" from fold, **Fig 9**.

Fig 9

8. Place fabric 3 right side down even with just-trimmed edge, **Fig 10**.

Fig 10

9. Turn foundation to marked side and sew along line between spaces 2 and 3; begin and end sewing 2 or 3 stitches beyond line, **Fig 11**.

Fig 11

10. Turn foundation over, open piece 3 and finger press seam, **Fig 12**. Glue or pin in place.

Fig 12

11. Turn foundation with marked side facing you; fold foundation forward along line between spaces 1, 3 and 4. If previous stitching makes it difficult to fold foundation forward, pull paper foundation away from fabric at stitching, then fold along line. If using a fabric foundation, fold it forward as far as it will go and trim to about ¼" from drawn line, **Fig 13**.

Fig 13

12. Sew along line between spaces 1, 3 and 4, **Fig 14**.

Fig 14

13. Continue trimming and sewing pieces in numerical order until block is complete, **Fig 15**. Press block, then trim fabric even with outside line of foundation to complete block, **Fig 16**.

Fig 15

Fig 16

Planning a Quilt

The variety of sizes of the Log Cabin blocks in this book allows for a wide range of quilts sizes. You can make small wall hangings as well as bed quilts.

Wall Hangings

To make a wall hanging, you can place sixteen blocks together and get the following sizes (without borders):

4" blocks for a 16" x 16" quilt

5" blocks for a 20" x 20" quilt

6" blocks for a 24" x 24" quilt

7" blocks for a 28" x 28" quilt

6" x 8" blocks for a 24" x 32" quilt

The blocks can be placed in a variety of settings, **Fig 17**.

Fig 17
Barn Raising

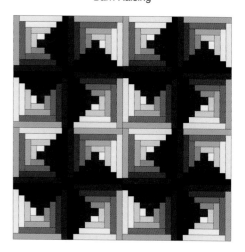

Fig 17
Sunshine and Shadows

Fig 17
Straight Furrows

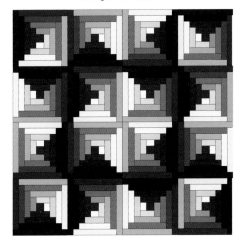

Fig 17
Star

Bed Quilts

Determine the size bed quilt you are making using the following chart as a guide.

Bed Size	Mattress Size
Crib	27" x 51"
Twin	39" x 75"
Double	54" x 75"
Queen	60" x 80"
King	76" x 80"

To the mattress size, add the desired drop (the part of the quilt that hangs over the edge of the mattress). If a tuck is desired (the part that is tucked under the pillows), also add that amount. For example, if you want your quilt to hang 12" over the edge of the mattress with a 12" tuck, add 24" to the length and width of the mattress size.

Once you have figured out how big your quilt will have to be, you will need to choose your block(s). If you use 7" square blocks, and want a traditional Log Cabin look, use 96

blocks (# 92) set 8 across and 12 down with a 2" and a 6" border to make a quilt with a finished size of 72" x 100", **Fig 18.**

Fig 18
Quilt Layout 1

Or, you can make a quilt with the rectangular 7" x 8" block (#37) and use only 80 blocks set 8 across and 10 down with a 2" and a 6" border to make a quilt with a finished size of 72" x 96", **Fig 19**.

Fig 19
Quilt Layout 2

7

Some of the square Log Cabin blocks can be set on point. If you use a 7" block, cut two 5½" squares in half diagonally and sew the triangles onto each side of the block, **Fig 20**. The block will now have a finished size of 9⅞".

Fig 20
Block #86

For a quilt with the new block size, you could use 48 blocks set 6 across and 8 down with a 3" and a 6" border to make a quilt with a finished size of 77¼" x 97", **Fig 21**.

With the same block, you could add 2" sashing strips and only use 35 blocks set 5 across and 7 down with 2" and 5" borders to make a quilt with a finished size of 71⅜" x 95⅛", **Fig 22**.

Fig 22
Quilt Layout 4

Fig 21
Quilt Layout 3

For quilts in other bed sizes, follow the quilt layouts in **Figs 18 to 22** and see chart below.

Layout	Twin	Full	Queen	King
Quilt Layout 1	60" x 102"	74" x 102"	80" x 108"	96" x 110"
• 3" and 6" borders (twin & full)	6 x 12	8 x 12	8 x 12	10 x 12
• 3", 4", 5" borders (queen)	72 blocks	96 blocks	96 blocks	120 blocks
• 3", 4", 6" borders (king)				
Quilt Layout 2	72" x 96"	72" x 96"	81" x 98"	95" x 98"
• 2" and 6" borders (twin & full)	8 x 10	8 x 10	9 x 10	11 x 10
• 3" and 6" borders (queen & king)	80 blocks	80 blocks	90 blocks	110 blocks
Quilt Layout 3	57½" x 97"	77¼" x 97"	81⅛" x 100⅞"	100⅞" x 100⅞"
• 3" and 6" borders (twin & full)	4 x 8	6 x 8	7 x 9	9 x 9
• 6" border (queen & king)	32 blocks	48 blocks	63 blocks	81 blocks
Quilt Layout 4	59½" x 95⅛"	71⅜" x 95⅛"	81¼" x 105"	105" x 105"
• 2" sashing and 2" & 5" borders(twin and full)	4 x 7	5 x 7	6 x 8	8 x 8
•2" sashing and 2" & 4" borders (queen & king)	28 blocks	35 blocks	48 blocks	64 blocks

Making Non-Traditional Log Cabin Quilts

While designing the blocks for this book, we took the concept of strips (logs) sewn around a center, and used it to create many different blocks with a contemporary look. Some sample quilt layouts using contemporary blocks are shown here, **Fig 23**.

Fig 23
Block #10

Fig 23
Block #12

Fig 23
Blocks #44, 45, 55 or 70

Fig 23
Blocks #44, 45, 55 or 70

9

There are also several blocks that have a small block as the center square. Using these blocks together in a quilt can provide a unique quilt with a country look, **Fig 24**.

Fig 24
Blocks 30, 61 and 87

Use the examples we've shown to plan your quilt or plan a completely different quilt. These 101 blocks are like a child's building blocks. You never know what you'll create until you start building.

Making the Quilt Top

Sew blocks (and sashing) in rows; sew rows together.

Measure quilt top lengthwise; cut two border strips to that length and sew to sides of quilt. Measure quilt top crosswise, including borders just added and cut two border strips to that length. Sew to top and bottom of quilt top. Repeat for any remaining borders.

If used, remove paper or non-woven backing at this time. **Hint:** Use a spray bottle of water to dampen paper for easier removal.

Marking the Quilting Design

Before marking on your quilt top, be sure to test any marking material to make sure it will wash out of your fabric. Mark all quilting lines on the right side of the fabric. For marking, use a hard lead pencil, chalk or other special quilt marking materials. If you quilt right on the marked lines, they will not show.

A word of caution: Marking lines which are intended to disappear after quilting—either by exposure to air or with water—may become permanent when set with a hot iron. Therefore, don't iron your quilt top after you have marked your quilting pattern.

If you are quilting around shapes, you may not need to mark the lines if you feel that you can accurately gauge the quilting line as you work. If you are quilting "in the ditch" of the seam (the space right in the seam), marking is not necessary. Any other quilting will need to be marked.

If you plan to tie your quilt, you do not need to mark it.

Attaching the Batting and Backing

There are a number of different types of batting on the market. Choose the one that is right for your quilt. Very thin cotton batting will require a great deal of quilting to hold it (quilting lines no more than 1" apart); very thick batting should be used only for tied quilts. A medium-loft bonded polyester batting is a good choice for machine quilting.

Hint: Remove batting from its packaging a day in advance and open it out full size. This will help the batting to lie flat.

Use 100% cotton fabric for the backing of your quilt. Bed sheets are usually not good backing materials. If you are making a bed-sized quilt, you will most likely have to piece your fabric to fit the quilt top. Cut off the selvages and sew pieces together carefully; press seams open. This is the only time in making a quilt that seams should be pressed open. Cut batting and backing about 2" larger than the quilt top on all sides. Place backing, wrong side up, on a flat surface. Place batting centered on top of backing, then center quilt right side up on batting.

The layers of the quilt must now be held together before quilting. There are three methods: thread basting, safety pin basting and quilt gun basting.

For thread basting, baste with long stitches, starting in the center and sewing toward the edges in a number of diagonal lines.

For safety pin basting, pin through all layers at once starting from the center and working out to the edges. Place the pins no more than 4" to 6" apart. Think of your quilt plan as you work and make certain that your pins avoid the prospective quilting lines. Choose rust-proof pins that are #1 or #2. To make pinning easier, many quilters use a quilter's spoon. The spoon is notched so that it can push the points of the safety pins closed.

For quilt gun basting, use the handy trigger tool (found in quilt and fabric stores) that pushes nylon tags through all layers of the quilt. Start in the center and work randomly toward the outside edges. Place tags about 4" apart. You can sew right over the tags and then they can be easily removed by cutting off with a pair of scissors.

Quilting

Your quilt can be either machine or hand quilted. *Note: Hand quilting may be a little more difficult if fabric or muslin was used as a foundation since there is an extra layer of fabric to quilt through. If you have never used a sewing machine for quilting, you might want to read more about the technique. Quilting for People Who Don't Have Time to Quilt, Book #4111 by Marti Michell and A Beginner's Guide to Machine Quilting,*

Book #4121 by Judi Tyrell, both published by ASN Publishing, are excellent introductions to machine quilting. These books are available at your local quilt store or department, or write the publisher for a list of sources.

You do not need a special machine for quilting. You can machine quilt with almost any home sewing machine. Just make sure that it is oiled and in good working condition. An even-feed foot is a good investment if you are going to machine quilt since it is designed to feed the top and bottom layers of the quilt through the machine evenly.

Use fine transparent nylon thread in the top and regular sewing thread in the bobbin.

To quilt in the ditch of a seam (this is actually stitching in the space between two pieces of fabric that have been sewn together), use your fingers to pull the blocks or pieces apart and machine stitch right between the two pieces. Try to keep your stitching just to the side of the seam that does not have the bulk of the seam allowance under it. When you have finished stitching, the quilting will be practically hidden in the seam.

Free form machine quilting is done with a darning foot and the feed dogs down on your sewing machine. It can be used to quilt around a design or to quilt a motif. Mark your quilting design as described in Marking the Quilting Design on page 10. Free form machine quilting takes practice to master because you are controlling the quilt through the machine rather than the machine moving the quilt. With free form machine quilting, you can quilt in any direction—up and down, side to side and even in circles without pivoting the quilt around the needle.

Attaching the Binding

Place the quilt on a flat surface and carefully trim the backing and batting $1/2$" beyond the quilt top edge. Measure the quilt top and cut two $2^1/2$"-wide binding strips the length of your quilt (for sides). Fold strips in half lengthwise wrong sides together. Place one strip along one side of the quilt; sew with a $1/4$" seam allowance, **Fig 25**. (Seam allowance should be measured from outer edge of quilt top fabric, not outer edge of batting/backing.)

Fig 25

Turn binding to back and slipstitch to backing covering previous stitching line, **Fig 26**. Repeat on other side.

Fig 26

For top and bottom edges, measure quilt crosswise and cut two $2^1/2$"-wide strips that size, adding $1/2$" to each end. Fold strips in half lengthwise with wrong sides together. Place one strip along top edge with $1/2$" extending beyond each side; sew with a $1/4$" seam allowance, **Fig 27**. Turn binding to back and tuck the extra $1/2$" under at each end; slipstitch to backing fabric.

Fig 27

The Finishing Touch

When your quilt is finished, always sign and date it. A label can be cross stitched, embroidered or even written with a permanent marking pen. Hand stitch to back of quilt.

1 Crazy Rose

Sunburst

3 Log Cabin Windows

4 Wreath in the Cabin

Hourglass

20	16	12	8	4		1		5	9	13	17	21

18

14

10

6

2

3

7

11

15

19

6 Dream House

8 Kaleidoscope

9 Medium Pineapple

10 Dorothy's Cabin

11 Pineapple Prism

12 **Twirling Ribbon**

13 Log Cabin Mudslide

14 Birdhouse Pentagon

15 Vertigo

16 Sweetheart Log Cabin

17 Cat in the Cabin

Photographed block note: *The cat's face was hand embroidered with three strands of embroidery floss as follows: eyes with green, nose with pink and mouth with dark gray.*

18 Bird in Flight

29

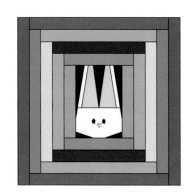

19 Bunny in the Cabin

Photographed block note: *The bunny's face was hand embroidered with three strands of embroidery floss as follows: eyes with dark gray and nose with pink.*

20 Diamond

21 Rolling Logs

22 Thick-and-Thin

23 Splitting Headache

24 Brilliant Rose

25 Slanted View

26 Rectangle Pineapple

27 *Perfectly Uneven Rectangle*

```
        14
       10
      6
    2
  17  13    9    5    1    3    7   11  15
    4
      8
       12
        16
```

30 Pine Tree in a Cabin

31 Wide-and-Narrow

32 *Five Hills in the Cabin*

33 Iridescent Diamond

34 Half a Pineapple

35 *Through the Cabin Door*

			16						
			12						
				8					
				4					
17	13	9	5	1	3	7	11	15
				2					
				6					
			10						
			14						

36 Courthouse Corners

37 Tall Log Cabin

					14				
				10					
				6					
				2					
17	13	9	5	1	3	7	11	15
				4					
				8					
				12					
				16					

38 Urban Log Cabin

39 Medium Center in the Corner

13						
11						
9						12
7					10	
5				8		
3		6				
1	2	4				

40 Courthouse Steps in a Cabin

41 **Abstract Flower**

42 Ornament in a Cabin

43 Small Pineapple

44 Small Curved Log Cabin

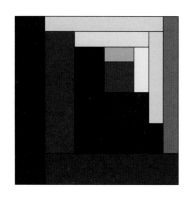

45 Large Curved Log Cabin

	10		
	6		
	2		
3	1	5	
7			9
11	4		13
	8		
	12		

Log Cabin in a Cabin

47 Log Cabin Pinwheel

48 Small Log Cabin

49 Cathedral Steps

20													
16													
12													
8													
4													
18	14	10	6	2	1	3	7	11	15	19			
5													
9													
13													
17													
21													

50 *Small Courthouse Steps*

					16					
					12					
					8					
					4					
14	10	6	2	1		3	7	11	15	
					5					
					9					
					13					
					17					

51 Skewed Window

52 Log A-Frame

53 Medium Log Cabin

```
        ┌──────────────────────────────┐
        │            10                │
        │  ┌────────────────────────┐  │
        │  │          6             │  │
        │  │  ┌──────────────────┐  │  │
        │  │  │        2       │  │  │  │
        │  │  │  ┌──────────┐  │  │  │  │
   13   │  9  │  5  │   1    │ 3 │ 7 │ 11 │
        │  │  │  └──────────┘  │  │  │  │
        │  │  │        4       │  │  │  │
        │  │  └──────────────────┘  │  │
        │  │          8             │  │
        │  └────────────────────────┘  │
        │            12                │
        └──────────────────────────────┘
```

54 Small Center in the Corner

55 *Medium Curved Log Cabin*

56 Spinning Log Cabin

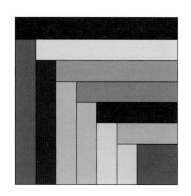

57 Large Center in the Corner

```
┌─────────────────────────────────────────────────┐
│                      13                           │
├──────────────────────────────────────┬───────────┤
│                  11                   │           │
├───────────────────────────┬──────────┤           │
│            9              │           │           │
├──────────────────┬────────┤           │           │
│        7         │        │    10     │    12     │
├───────────┬──────┤    8   │           │           │
│     5     │      │        │           │           │
├──────┬────┤  6   │        │           │           │
│  3   │    │      │        │           │           │
├───┬──┤  4 │      │        │           │           │
│ 1 │2 │    │      │        │           │           │
└───┴──┴────┴──────┴────────┴───────────┴───────────┘
```

58 Diamond in the Cabin

59 Medium Courthouse Steps

60 *Pineapple in the Cabin*

Heart of
the Cabin

62 Large Courthouse Steps

						24							
						20							
						16							
						12							
						8							
						4							
22	18	14	10	6	2	1	3	7	11	15	19	23
						5							
						9							
						13							
						17							
						21							
						25							

63 Tumbling Rectangle Log Cabin

65 Toppling Log Cabin

66 All Around the Cabin

67 Crazy Cabin

68 Guardian Angel

Photographed block note: *Eyes were hand embroidered with three strands of blue-gray floss.*

69 Curved Log Cabin Tulip

70 Petite Curved Log Cabin

		10		
		6		
		2		
11	7	3 1	5	9	13
		4		
	8			
12				

71 Half-Square Triangle in the Cabin

72 Cabin in the Meadow

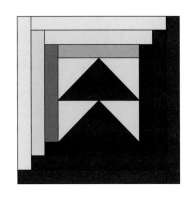

73 Geese in the Cabin

74 Rectangle in the Corner

The block diagram shows numbered pieces arranged in a log-cabin style corner layout:

14

12

10

8

6

15

13

11

4

9

7

2

5

3

1

75 Petite Center in the Corner

```
                    11

                    9

              7

          5

     3

1        2      4    6    8    10
```

Evening Star

Log Cabin Community

78 Skyscraper Steps

						20						
						16						
						12						
						8						
18	14	10	6			4			7	11	15	19
				2	1		3					
						5						
						9						
						13						
						17						
						21						

80 Double Diamonds

82 Square in a Square Log Cabin

83 Blooming Log Cabin

84 Log Cabin with a View

85 House in a Twister

86 Cactus Flower

87 Cabin in the Cabin

88 Petite Courthouse Steps

```
                    12

              8

         4

    2    1    3
10  6             7  11

         5

              9

                    13
```

89 Off-Center Quartet

90 Birdhouse in the Cabin

92 Large Log Cabin

93 Petite Pineapple

94 Hexagon Log Cabin

95 Spiral Staircase

96 Pineapple on Point

97 **Flower Basket**

98 Log Cabin Playhouse

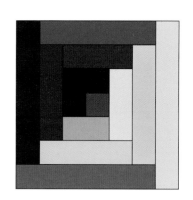

					10			
				6				
				2				
13	9	5		1	3	7	11
				4				
				8				
				12				

99 Curved Log Cabin Nosegay

100 Home with Siding

101 Two-Story Log Cabin

							16						

12

8

4

14 | 10 | 6 | 2 | 1 | 3 | 7 | 11 | 15

5

9

13

17